Our Loving God

Our Loving God

This book was given with love

to: _____

from: _____

on: _____

The Lord is righteous
in all his ways
and loving towards
all he has made.

Psalm 145 verse 17

Our Loving God

Carine Mackenzie

CHRISTIAN FOCUS

© Christian Focus
Published in 1997 by Christian Focus Publications Ltd.
Geanies House, Fearn, Tain, Ross-shire, IV20 1TW, Scotland.

Written by Carine Mackenzie
Illustrations by Fred Apps

Casebound edition ISBN 1-85792-294-8
Limpbound edition ISBN 1-85792-419-3

CONTENTS

1 WHO GOD IS

2 WHAT GOD DOES

3 WHAT GOD GIVES

4 WHAT GOD ASKS FROM US

WHO GOD IS

We learn about God in his Word - the Bible. God is a Spirit. He does not have a body like we have. We cannot see him but he is very real. We do not see the wind either - but we can see the effects of the wind.

God is so great and powerful - more than we can understand.

God had no beginning as we did. He has no end either. God never changes. He was, is and always will be wise, holy, true and loving.

God Made the World

God created the world and everything that is in it from nothing. He spoke a few words and the different parts of creation came into being. He did this in six days and rested on the seventh day.

On the first day
he created light.

On the second day
he made the atmosphere,
and the waters that are in
the oceans, and rivers.

On the third day
God spoke and made the dry
land - the beautiful mountains,
valleys, islands and deserts.
He made the trees, bushes,
cacti and flowers. God was
pleased with what
he had made.

6

On the fourth day
God made the sun,
moon and stars.

On the fifth day
he made the sea creatures
and birds.

On the sixth day
God made the animals - the
leopard, deer, the pig and the
elephant.

Then came his special creation -
'Let us make man in our own image,'
God said. 'He will rule over the fish
and the birds and the animals.'
God made human beings - the man
he called Adam and his wife Eve.

God is in control

God made the world and is in control of it. The earth moves once round the sun every year giving us the seasons - God is in control. The earth spins on its axis every 24 hours - giving us days and nights. God does this too.

When a seed is planted in the ground, God causes the corn to grow.

When a bulb is planted in the garden, God causes the daffodil to grow.

God gives us the spring time for planting and the harvest time. Without his power there would be no crops. God gave the animals and the birds and fish the ability to produce little ones.

Every day the oceans rise and fall with the movement of the tides. God is in control.

Our bodies are very complicated. Through God's power our hearts beat, our lungs breathe, our ears hear and our eyes see.

People have spoiled God's beautiful, perfect creation by sin. The first people, Adam and Eve, sinned against God and so everybody born into this world is a sinner.

God still loves and cares for his world. He loved the world so much that he sent his Son Jesus to take away the sin of the world. We can now become right with God.

9

3 persons = 1 God

The Bible tells us that there is only one God. However it speaks of three different persons in this one God:

> God the Father,
> God the Son,
> and God the Holy Spirit

These three persons are each God: yet although they are equal, they each do different things.

God the Father sent the Son to be the Saviour. God the Son became a man and died for our sins, was buried and rose again from the dead. We call him Jesus Christ.

God the Holy Spirit was Christ's helper. He is our helper too and causes people to be born into the family of God.

When Jesus, the Son of God, was living and working in this world, he went one day to the River Jordan. There he met John the Baptist and asked him to baptize him. John did not want to do this at first. He did not feel worthy. But Jesus persuaded him that it was the right thing to do.

When the Lord Jesus, God the Son, came up out of the water of the River Jordan, the heavens opened up. God the Holy Spirit came down on him, shaped like a dove.

God the Father spoke from heaven saying, 'This my beloved Son, with whom I am well pleased.'

WHAT GOD DOES

God is living and true. He is just and fair in his judgement; he hates sin and punishes sinful actions, words and thoughts. But God is merciful and gracious to those who confess their sin and come to him through the Lord Jesus Christ.

God is a loving Father who guides, teaches and corrects his children and who comforts them when they are upset.

God is all-powerful and with him all things are possible.

Through the ages he has guided his people, and he still guides them today, by his Word and by the things that happen in their lives. The boy or girl who trusts and follows him will be directed by God.

God Guides His People

Abraham was a friend of God. When he lived in Haran, God spoke to him and told him to go on a long journey to a new land. God promised to be with him and to bless him. Abraham obeyed God and set out on his long journey.

Many years later when his son Isaac was grown-up, Abraham called his chief servant and said to him, 'I want you to go back to Haran to find a young woman to be my son Isaac's wife.'

The servant thought that would be a very difficult task. Abraham assured him that God would guide him.

The servant went on the long journey back to Haran with ten camels laden with lovely gifts. He stopped beside a water spring and prayed to God. 'Please give me success and show kindness to my master Abraham. When the girls come to fetch water at this spring, please lead me to the one that is to be Isaac's wife. If one of the girls offers to fetch water, not only for me but also for my camels, may she be the one that you have chosen.'

Abraham's servant asked God for this special sign to guide him to the right girl. God heard his request graciously. Before he had even finished praying, Rebekah came to the well. He hurried up to her and asked her for a drink of water. She gladly gave him some and then said, ' I'll draw some water for your camels too.' His prayer was answered.

Silently he watched as Rebekah continued with her tasks. He was sure that God had guided him to the right girl. Before he went to see her father and family, he bowed down and thanked God for his goodness.

He realised that he had not found Rebekah because of his own cleverness but because God had led him as he went faithfully about his work, asking God for his help.

God still guides his people through his Word, the Bible, which tells us how to live. He guides us too in the things which happen from day to day.

God Comforts His People

God's love for his people is a wonderful comfort to them when they are unhappy or in trouble. God is called the God of all comfort.

The Lord Jesus met a sick lady one day. She had been ill for 12 years - slowly bleeding inside. She had gone to lots of doctors and spent all her savings looking for a cure. They had not been able to help her.

She saw Jesus in a crowd of people and crept up to him and touched the edge of his robe. Immediately the bleeding stopped - she was cured.

'Who touched me?' Jesus asked.

Nobody admitted it. One of Jesus' disciples, Peter, said, 'Master, there are so many people crowding around, somebody was bound to touch you.'

'No,' replied Jesus, 'someone touched me on purpose. I felt my healing power being used.'

The lady heard this conversation and she was afraid. She began to tremble and fell down on her knees in front of Jesus.

'I touched you,' she said, 'and now I am well.'

Jesus was not angry with her. He immediately spoke comforting words to her. 'Daughter,' he called her, 'your faith has healed you. Go in peace.'

How happy and comforted she must have felt, to hear the encouraging and strengthening words of the Lord Jesus.

God's Word is full of comforting words to those who love and trust him. 'Do not let your hearts be troubled. Trust in God.'

God Corrects His People

God hates sin. When his people sin, God as a loving Father, must point out that sin to them and correct them.

King David was a follower of God, but he sinned terribly - ignoring God's commandments and going his own way. To make matters worse he seemed to be unaware that what he had done was wrong.

Because he was one of God's children, God sent a messenger to him to confront him with his sin and to put him right.

The man God sent to David was Nathan the prophet. Nathan went to King David and told him a story.

'There were two men in the city - one rich and one poor. The rich man had lots of sheep, but the poor man had only one pet lamb. He and his family were very fond of the lamb. One day the rich man had an important visitor. He wanted to prepare a nice dish of roast lamb, but instead of using one of his own, he took the little pet lamb belonging to the poor man.'

When David heard the story, he was furious. How could any man do such a mean thing? He would deal very severely with that rich man.

Then Nathan faced David and said 'You are that man!' David was shocked.

'God has given you so much. Yet you had Uriah killed so that you could have his wife for yourself.'

David's serious sin suddenly dawned on him and he asked for God's forgiveness.

God heard David's prayer and forgave him. We too are sinners by nature and sin every day. If we confess our sin to God and ask him to forgive us, he will cleanse us because God the Son has taken the punishment for his people's sin when he died on the cross.

WHAT GOD GIVES

We all love to receive presents. God is the most loving and generous present giver. Do we realise that he has provided us with so many things? Do we remember to say, 'Thank you'?

Our food, our family, our homes - all these have been given to us by God.

God's Word - the Bible - is a very special gift. God's day of rest - the Lord's day - is also a precious gift from God.

God's most special and loving gift is his Son - the Lord Jesus Christ, God the Son.

'For God loved the world so much that he gave his only Son, so that everyone who believes in him may not die but have eternal life.'
(John 3 v 16)

God gives us Home and Family

You were born into a family - perhaps you have brothers or sisters, aunts uncles and cousins. Our relatives and friends are given to us by God.

Many people live in comfortable homes where they are loved and cared for. This too is a gift from God. Yet there are also lots of people in our world who do not have such a wonderful gift.

Ruth was a lovely young woman who lived in the land of Moab. She got married to a young man who had come with his parents and brother from Bethlehem. But sadly Ruth's husband and his father and brother died. Ruth and her mother-in-law, Naomi and her sister-in-law were left on their own.

Naomi decided it would be wise to go back to her home town of Bethlehem - a long way away. Ruth insisted on coming with her - 'Don't ask me to leave you,' she pleaded with Naomi. 'I want to go and stay with you. Your people will be my people and your God will be my God.'

So Ruth and Naomi - both widows - made a sad journey to Bethlehem. They set up home together. There was no man in the house to provide for them - so Ruth went out to the harvest fields to gather the left-over ears of corn and provided food for herself and her mother-in-law.

Boaz, the owner of the field, was a relative of Naomi's husband. He went to a great deal of trouble to make sure that Ruth was able to gather grain, and that she was well provided for at meal times.

But Boaz cared for Ruth in a very special way - he made her his wife. They became a family and had children of their own. Naomi lived with them too and helped to look after the children.

God provided Ruth with a family and a lovely home. He still provides for each one of us today.

God Gives us His Word

God has given us a marvellous gift of the book we call the Bible.
This book is made up of 66 smaller books - some history books,
some letters. It was written over many hundreds of years by
many different people who all loved the Lord God. God the Holy
Spirit put the right words into their minds so that they did not
make any mistakes.

One part of the Bible was written by God himself on two tablets
of stone given to his servant Moses. These are the 10
Commandments that tell us how to live. It is our duty to obey
God's commandments.

Not everybody listens to what God is telling them in his Word.
Jeremiah, one of God's messengers, wrote part of God's Word.
He wrote telling the people to stop sinning, or God would punish
them.

24

When the king heard these words being read he was angry. He snatched the scroll, cut it up with a pen knife and threw the pieces into the fire.

But God's Word was not completely destroyed. Jeremiah wrote the message again and we still have these words in the book of Jeremiah.

Jesus, the Son of God, tells us that, 'Heaven and earth will disappear but my words will remain forever.'

God's Word is a guide for our lives, like a light showing us the way along a dark road.

God Gives Us a Day of Rest

When God created the earth he did all the work in six days and rested on the seventh day. He did that, not because he was tired, but as an example to us.

One of the commandments written on the stone tablet by God is, 'Remember the Sabbath day by keeping it holy. Six days you shall labour and do all your work, but the seventh day is a Sabbath to the Lord your God.'

The Lord Jesus Christ rose from the dead on the first day of the week, and from then on we call this day the Christian Sabbath or the Lord's day. This is a special day when we meet together in God's house to worship him.

Lydia was a business woman who worked in Philippi, but she stopped her work on the Sabbath day to meet her friends to pray together. Paul went to this gathering on one of his journeys and preached to the people. Lydia was affected by the word preached by Paul and she trusted in the Lord Jesus.

God tells us that the Lord's day is a day of rest, but some work is necessary. Jesus healed sick people on the Sabbath day.

Today, too, there are some jobs that have to be done on the Lord's day. But the Lord's day is God's special day which should be a delight to us.

God Gave us His Son

God sent his Son from heaven to this world. God the Son was equal in power and glory with God the Father and God the Holy Spirit. God the Son became a baby in Bethlehem about 2,000 years ago. His name was Jesus.

The Lord Jesus showed his love for people in many ways - he healed sick people, he made blind people see again, he even raised some dead people to life, he told wonderful stories, he loved to see little children too.

The most amazing event that showed his great love for people happened at Calvary, outside Jerusalem. The Lord Jesus, God the Son, was put to death on a cross. He suffered so much pain and agony and then died. Jesus loved his people so much that he took this agony and death as a punishment for all their sins. The holy God could now say to his people, 'Your sins have been punished already. My Son took the punishment. You are forgiven.'

Three days after his death, Jesus came back to life. Some of his friends came to the tomb where he was buried, expecting to see Jesus' body. Instead they saw an angel, who spoke to them, 'Don't be afraid. Jesus is not here, he has risen.'

What wonderful news for them! They met Jesus again and he spent time with them during the next 40 days.

One day when they were out on a mountain top near Jerusalem, Jesus went up through the clouds back into heaven. He is there today, still loving his friends in this world and praying for them. How we should love him!

God Will Give Us Heaven

Stephen loved God and worked hard to serve God in the church as a deacon. He had a responsible position managing the business affairs of the church in Jerusalem. He spoke out boldly for the Lord Jesus God gave him special power to do many miraculous things.

The leaders of the Synagogue did not like to hear Stephen telling the people about the Lord Jesus. This teaching turned their own ideas upside down. They argued with him but Stephen's words were wise. They could not get the better of him. God was helping him.

Then they got someone to tell lies about him. He was arrested and taken to the chief Jewish court.

Stephen looked up to heaven and saw in a vision Jesus standing at the right hand of God. He told his accusers what he saw. This made them even angrier. They rushed at him, shouting and yelling and dragged him out of the city and threw huge stones at him. Just before he died Stephen prayed to the Lord, 'Lord Jesus, receive my spirit.'

He asked God to forgive the men who were throwing stones at him. Stephen then died and his spirit went to heaven to be with the Lord Jesus.

Heaven is promised to all who believe in Jesus. We cannot fully understand how wonderful it will be. The Lord Jesus will be there to welcome his children just as he welcomed Stephen.

WHAT GOD ASKS
FROM US

God tells us about himself in his Word, the Bible.

He tells us that he loves us, so that, *we can love him too.*

He tells us that he is holy and wise and powerful, so that, *we can worship him.*

He speaks to us in his word, and *he wants us to speak to him in prayer.*

God's actions requires a response from us.

We Should Give God Love

God shows amazing love to his people by his kindness and care. We ought to love
Lord God with all our heart, and mind, and soul and strength. And if we love him
do so because he has first loved us and put his love in our hearts.

One day Jesus was having a meal in the home of Simon, a synagogue leader. A
lady heard that Jesus was there. She had led a sinful life. Simon did not appro
her.

The lady was crying so much, her tears washed Jesus' feet. She wiped them
her hair. She brought a beautiful alabaster jar of perfume - her
treasured possession - and poured this
beautiful perfume on Jesus' feet.

Simon was angry that Jesus would
allow such a woman to touch his feet. But
Jesus explained to him, 'You did not wash
my feet, as is the custom, when I came
into your home. This woman washed my
feet with her tears. You did not put oil on
my head, she put perfume on my feet. She
has loved me very much, because her
many sins have been forgiven.'

Her love to God was shown in a practical
way - by giving her best gift to the Lord
Jesus.

How can we show our love to God? One
way is by showing love to his people, by
caring for them, by helping others in need,
by visiting people who are sick. Jesus said
that if we have given help and love to even
the least important of his people, it is as if
we have given it to him.

We should Obey God

Noah and his wife and family lived long, long ago. Noah was a good man who listened to what God said to him. The people who lived in his district were evil and violent. God was displeased with their sins

God decided to cover the earth with a flood of water to destroy everything and everyone that was evil. But he warned Noah and told him to build a huge boat (called an ark) so that he and his wife and family would be safe when the flood came. Noah was to take a pair of each kind of animal too.

Noah's neighbours thought he was crazy building an enormous boat. Noah did everything just as God commanded him. It was more important to him to obey God than to listen to evil men.

When God did send a flood, Noah and his family were ready. They were saved from a terrible disaster by obeying God.

God wants us to obey him too. He has given us his commandments. People will tell us, as they told Noah, that it is silly to obey God's commandments, but we too should obey God rather than men. God has promised blessing to those who obey his Word.

We cannot keep his laws perfectly, and often do things that are wrong. We must ask God to help us, and to forgive us when we go wrong. He has promised to be kind and merciful.

We Should Pray to God

When we pray, we are not speaking to ourselves or to other people who may be in the room with us. We are speaking to God.

God loves to hear his children asking him, humbly, from the heart for things that are good. Our prayer does not need to be long. God hears short prayers too.

Jesus told a story about two men who went to the temple to pray. One was a Pharisee, a religious man. He prayed, full of pride about his own achievements. 'Thank you God, that I am not like other wicked men. I fast twice a week and I give a tenth of my money to the temple collection.'

The other man was a tax-collector - although he had an important job, he was not popular. This man was ashamed of his behaviour. He prayed, 'God, have mercy on me a sinner.' Just a short prayer, but Jesus tells us that the tax-collector's prayer was heard by God. He had humbled himself before God and God had answered his prayer and shown him mercy. He left the temple that day at peace with God.

God wants us to pray like that tax-collector - humbly asking for forgiveness. We can pray to God about everything. We should not be worried about anything, but thankfully pray to God about all our concerns.

OUR LOVING GOD

God - the Father, Son and Holy Spirit - is worthy of your worship and your love.

'No one has ever seen God but if we love one another, God lives in us and his love is made complete in us.'
(1 John 4 v 12)

Other titles

by Carine Mackenzie

The Life of Jesus

Who is Jesus? What did he do? What's he really like? Have you ever asked questions like these? Do you want to know more about Jesus and all the things he said and did? This book will help you to find out more than just what Jesus did 2,000 years ago. It will tell you what he is doing now and how you can get to know him.

ISBN 0 906731 89 5

Jesus and his Kingdom

Jesus is the master storyteller. Read this book and you will discover this for yourself. He uses everyday sights and activities to make his teachings about God's Kingdom simple and easy to remember. Jesus says that the Kingdom of God is in the hearts of men and women, boys and girls - read this book and find out about how you can be part of it too.

ISBN 1 871676 61 4

The Caring Creator

God is powerful. He made the whole world just by speaking! God is loving. He cares for the people, the plants and the animals which he made. God has a plan - to care for and renew his creation. Then the wolf and the lamb will be friends; the lions will be as tame as the horses and cows. Read this book to discover how you are part of God's plan and how we should trust him and tell others about him.

ISBN 1 85792 071 6

Children of the Bible

Children are in the Bible. They are everywhere. Read this book and find out the amazing ways that God has used children to fight giants, rule countries and to show his power! When you read this book you will discover a God who cares for children and loves them so much that he actually sent his own son, Jesus, to die for them.

ISBN 1 85792 032 5